FACT CAT

RAINFOREST

Izzi Howell

WAYLAND

FACT CAT

Get your paws on this fantastic new mega-series from Wayland!

Join our Fact Cat on a journey of fun learning about every subject under the sun!

First published in Great Britain in 2015 by Wayland
Copyright © Wayland 2015

Wayland
An imprint of Hachette Children's Group
Part of Hodder & Stoughton
Carmelite House
50 Victoria Embankment
London EC4Y 0DZ

ISBN: 978 0 7502 8219 2
ebook ISBN: 978 0 7502 9468 3
Dewey Number: 333.7'5-dc23

10 9 8 7 6 5 4 3 2 1

MIX
Paper from responsible sources
FSC® C104740

Editor: Izzi Howell
Design: Rocket Design (East Anglia) Ltd
Fact Cat illustrations: Shutterstock/Julien Troneur
Other illustrations: Stefan Chabluk
Consultant: Kate Ruttle

Produced for Wayland by
White-Thomson Publishing Ltd
www.wtpub.co.uk
+44 (0) 843 208 7460

An Hachette UK Company
www.hachette.co.uk
www.hachettechildrens.co.uk

Printed and bound in China

Picture and illustration credits:
Dreamstime: Rangizzz 14, Jaco Janse Van Rensburg 14, Palko72 14, Carlos Mora 16, Roland Nagy 20; Shutterstock: Wollertz cover, Colette3 title page, worldswildlifewonders 4 and 11, Dirk Ercken 4, kubais 4, Phil Robinson 4, Dr. Morley Read 5, Chris Humphries 7, Aimee McLachlan 8, Dobermaraner 9, Mark Bridger 11, kkaplin 12, AlessandroZocc 12, Arun Roisri 13, Dr. Morley Read 13, Det-anan 14, Panu Ruangjan 15, Amy Nichole Harris 17, Jiri Hera 18, ilovezion 19, Janelle Lugge 20, Matej Hudovernik 21; Stefan Chabluk: 5, 6; Thinkstock: pxhidalgo 4, Wendy Townrow 12, saiko3p 18, Dorling Kindersley 19; Visuals Unlimited/Science Photo Library: Joe McDonald 10

Every effort has been made to clear copyright. Should there be any inadvertent omission, please apply to the publisher for rectification.

The author, Izzi Howell, is a writer and editor specialising in children's educational publishing.

The consultant, Kate Ruttle, is a literacy expert and SENCO, and teaches in Suffolk.

FACT CAT FACT

There is a question for you to answer on each spread in this book. You can check your answers on page 24.

CONTENTS

WHAT IS A RAINFOREST?

A rainforest is a hot, wet **habitat** full of **tropical** trees and plants. It rains almost every day in the rainforest.

Rainforests are home to millions of different types of plants and animals.

pit viper

banana flower

ferns

strawberry poison frog

There are rainforests along the **equator**, in places such as South America, central Africa and Southeast Asia.

The Amazon rainforest in Brazil is the biggest rainforest on the planet. It is bigger than most of the countries in the world! Find the Amazon on this map.

NORTH AMERICA

EUROPE

ASIA

AFRICA

Equator

SOUTH AMERICA

AUSTRALIA

Rainforest

FACT CAT FACT

The trees in the rainforest are so close together that it can take 10 minutes for a drop of rain to fall from the treetops to the ground.

THE LOWER LAYERS

There are four **layers** in a rainforest. Each layer forms a separate habitat. Different animals and plants live in each layer.

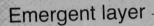

Emergent layer

Canopy

Understorey

Rainforest floor

The lowest layer is the muddy rainforest floor. It is very dark here because the trees stop the light coming through.

The second layer is called the understorey. This layer is under the tree leaves, but above the forest floor. Most plants grow up to this layer.

Big cats, such as jaguars and leopards, look for **prey** in the understorey. Find out the name of another big cat that lives in the rainforest.

FACT CAT **FACT**

The rainforest floor is home to many animals. Big, hairy spiders called tarantulas live in holes in the ground. Agoutis, which are similar to guinea pigs, live in **hollow** logs.

THE TOP LAYERS

The third layer is called the canopy. It is made of leaves and high branches. It stops sunshine reaching the forest floor and understorey.

These squirrel monkeys live in the canopy. They can find lots of fruit to eat here. The high branches give them **shelter** from big cats.

The top of the rainforest is called the emergent layer. This is the highest and sunniest part of the rainforest.

Only butterflies and birds can live in the emergent layer. Find out what butterflies eat.

FACT CAT **FACT**

Some rainforest trees are 46 metres tall. That's as tall as eight double-decker buses!

WILDLIFE

Most animals live high in the canopy of the rainforest, so they have to be good at moving between the trees.

Some animals without wings have even learned to **glide** between trees, like this sugar glider that lives in Australia.

FACT CAT FACT

Sugar gliders are **nocturnal**. This means that they sleep all day, and are awake all night.

Some animals in the rainforest use **camouflage** to hide. Other animals have very bright colours to show that they are **poisonous**.

This red-eyed tree frog catches insects to eat with its long sticky tongue. Find out if red-eyed tree frogs are poisonous.

Camouflage helps this green pit viper to hide in plants.

PLANTS

Most rainforest plants have their **roots** in the dark rainforest floor. They grow up into the understorey or canopy towards the sunlight.

The rafflesia flower is one of the biggest flowers in the world. Find out how much each flower weighs.

FACT CAT FACT

The pitcher plant has cup-shaped leaves that produce a sweet liquid to attract insects. When insects drink from the plant, they fall in and the plant eats them.

Tall rainforest trees need strong roots to support their height. **Buttress roots** grow above the ground and spread out over a large area to support the tree.

Tree roots give shelter to animals that live on the forest floor. **Tapirs** hide from big cats behind tall buttress roots.

tapir

buttress root

A FOOD CHAIN

Rainforest animals and plants get all their food from their habitat. Plants make their own food with the help of sunlight. Rainforest animals eat plants or other animals.

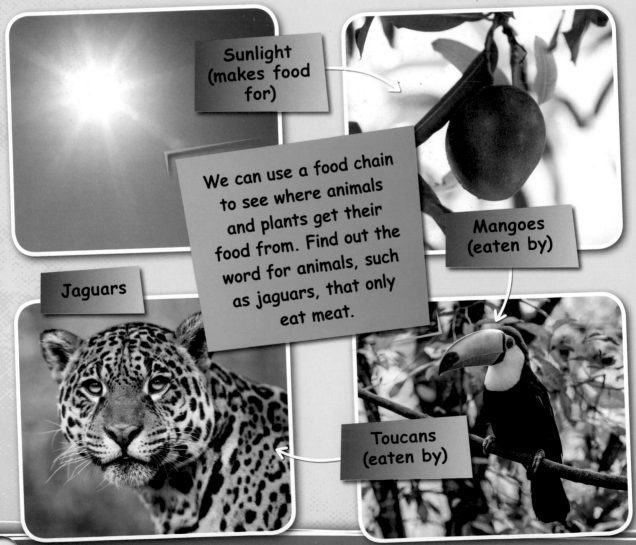

Sunlight (makes food for)

We can use a food chain to see where animals and plants get their food from. Find out the word for animals, such as jaguars, that only eat meat.

Mangoes (eaten by)

Jaguars

Toucans (eaten by)

Food chains show us how everything is connected in rainforests. For example, jaguars don't eat plants, but plants are still important to them. This is because jaguars eat toucans who need plants to survive.

This black-backed kingfisher will feed this spider to her young.

FACT CAT **FACT**

Toucans have big beaks. Their beaks are made of the same **material** as your hair and fingernails.

PEOPLE

Tribes of people live in the rainforests. They have lived there for thousands of years. Some tribes use rainforest plants to make food and furniture.

This boy is collecting fruit to eat or make into juice. His basket is made out of rainforest vines.

On special occasions, men from the Huli tribe paint their faces and wear **wigs**. Find out which country the Huli tribe live in.

In the Amazon, Yanomami tribes live together in houses called shabonos, made of leaves and logs. The living area is for everyone, but families have their own place to cook and sleep.

FACT CAT FACT

People think that there are around 80 tribes in the Amazon rainforest that have no contact with the outside world. They live deep in the rainforest.

PRODUCTS FROM THE RAINFOREST

We use **products** from the rainforest every day. Shampoo is made from rainforest plants such as coconuts. The vanilla flavour in ice cream comes from a rainforest flower.

Chocolate is made from the seeds of these yellow fruit. Find out the name of this plant.

Many of the medicines we use are made from rainforest plants and flowers. These medicines help people who have problems with their heart, skin and eyes.

Make-up is also made from rainforest plants. We use the seeds of the lipstick tree to make lipstick red.

The white liquid from this rainforest tree is used to make rubber. Rubber is the strong stretchy material that car **tyres** are made of.

tyre

PROTECTING THE RAINFORESTS

Cutting down trees, or **deforestation**, is the biggest danger to the rainforest. People cut down trees because they want to make things out of the wood, or use the land for farms or **mines**.

deforestation

These people are planting rainforest trees. They will grow into new rainforests.

replanting

When we cut down trees, we take away animals' habitats. Many types of animals are becoming **extinct** because their habitat is being **destroyed**.

Orang-utans are an **endangered** rainforest animal. Find out the name of another endangered rainforest animal.

FACT CAT **FACT**

If we continue to cut down the rainforest trees, there won't be any rainforests left in about 50 years. But if we all work together to **protect** the rainforests, we can help to save them.

QUIZ Try to answer the questions below. Look back through the book to help you. Check your answers on page 24.

1 The Amazon is the biggest rainforest in the world. True or not true?

a) true

b) not true

2 There are three layers in a rainforest. True or not true?

a) true

b) not true

3 Big cats can go into the emergent layer. True or not true?

a) true

b) not true

4 Poisonous animals are often brightly coloured. True or not true?

a) true

b) not true

5 Pitcher plants can eat humans. True or not true?

a) true

b) not true

6 Some homes in the rainforest are made out of plants. True or not true?

a) true

b) not true

GLOSSARY

buttress roots large roots that grow above the ground

camouflage hiding by making yourself the same colour as the area you are in

deforestation cutting down large areas of trees

destroyed damaged so badly that it doesn't exist anymore

endangered something that might become extinct if we don't protect it

equator an imaginary line that goes around the middle of the Earth

extinct something that doesn't live on Earth any more, such as dinosaurs

glide to move through the air without using wings

habitat the place where an animal or plant lives

hollow with an empty space inside

layers parts that go on top of each other

material what something is made of

mine a place where metal and rocks are dug out of the ground

nocturnal something that sleeps all day and is awake at night

poisonous can hurt or kill you if you eat or touch it

prey animals that other animals kill for food

product something that is made to be sold in shops

protect to keep something safe

roots the part of the tree that grows underground

shelter a safe place

tapir a type of wild rainforest pig

tribe a group of people who live together

tropical something from a hot part of the world near the Equator

tyre the black outside part of a car wheel

wig something we wear on our head that looks like hair

INDEX

ANSWERS

Pages 5–21

Page 5: In the north of South America

Page 7: Tigers, panthers and ocelots, but not lions, who live in the savannah

Page 9: Nectar, a sweet juice inside flowers

Page 11: No, they are not

Page 12: Up to 10 kilograms

Page 14: Carnivore

Page 17: Papua New Guinea

Page 18: The cacao tree

Page 21: Most rainforest animals, including gorillas, chimpanzees and manatees

Quiz answers

1 a) true

2 b) not true, there are four layers

3 b) not true, only birds and butterflies live in this layer

4 a) true

5 b) not true, they only eat insects

6 a) true

WAYLAND

OTHER TITLES IN THE FACT CAT SERIES...

SPACE

THE EARTH

978 0 7502 8220 8

THE MOON

978 0 7502 8221 5

THE PLANETS

978 0 7502 8222 2

THE SUN

978 0 7502 8223 9

UNITED KINGDOM

ENGLAND

978 0 7502 8433 2

NORTHERN IRELAND

978 0 7502 8440 0

SCOTLAND

978 0 7502 8439 4

WALES

978 0 7502 8438 7

COUNTRIES

BRAZIL

978 0 7502 8213 0

FRANCE

978 0 7502 8212 3

GHANA

978 0 7502 8215 4

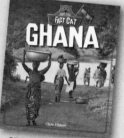

ITALY

978 0 7502 8214 7

HISTORY

NEIL ARMSTRONG
First Man on the Moon

978 0 7502 9040 1

AMELIA EARHART
Transatlantic Pilot

978 0 7502 9034 0

CHRISTOPHER COLUMBUS
Sailing to America

978 0 7502 9031 9

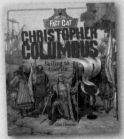

THE WRIGHT BROTHERS
First Flight

978 0 7502 9037 1